BUILDING a Heart of Faith

TALKING
ABOUT
GOD & JESUS
WITH
KIDS

Building a Heart of Faith:
Talking About God and Jesus With Kids

Requests for permission should be addressed in writing to Abingdon Press,
201 Eighth Avenue, South, P.O. Box 801, Nashville, TN 37203

ISBN: 978-0687-46496-8

PACP00415936-01

Writers: Marjorie Suchocki and Joan Lucas
Editor: LeeDell Stickler
Production Editor: Charlotte Overlay
Production and Design Manager: Philip Francis
Cover and Interior Design: Paige Easter

09 10 11 12 13 14 15 16 17 18—10 9 8 7 6 5 4 3 2 1

MANUFACTURED IN THE UNITED STATES OF AMERICA

TABLE OF CONTENTS

Introduction 05

How to Use This Book 06

Chapter 1: CREATION 07

The Basics for Parents & Teachers 07
The Bible Story: Genesis 1:1–2:4 (Creation) 09
A Story for Today: God's Call 11
Lighten Up: God Keeps Creating! 15
Lighten Up: Flower Power 16

Chapter 2: GOD'S PRESENCE 17

The Basics for Parents & Teachers 17
The Bible Story: Psalm 139 (God's Presence) 19
A Story for Today: The Footprint Hunt 21
Lighten Up: God & the Horsehead Nebula 25
Lighten Up: Where Is God? 26

Chapter 3: CHRISTMAS 27

The Basics for Parents & Teachers 27
The Bible Story: Luke 2:1-20 (Christmas) 29
A Story for Today: Love Came Down 32
Lighten Up: Ho Ho Ho 36

Chapter 4: STORIES JESUS TOLD 37

The Basics for Parents & Teachers 37
The Bible Story: Luke 10:25-37 (The Good Samaritan) . . .39
A Story for Today: The Visitors 42
Lighten Up: Googling God 46

Chapter 5: GOOD FRIDAY & EASTER 47

The Basics for Parents & Teachers 47
The Bible Story: John 17–20 (Crucifixion & Resurrection) . . .49
A Story for Today: Building Up 52
Lighten Up: God With Us 56

CHAPTER 6: GOOD TIMES & BAD 57

The Basics for Parents & Teachers 57
The Bible Story: Luke 15:11-32 (The Prodigal Son) 59
A Story for Today: Life Expectancy of Birds 62
Lighten Up: A Rock and a Hard Place 66

CHAPTER 7: GOD TRANSFORMS US 67

The Basics for Parents & Teachers 67
The Bible Story: Acts 9:1-20 (Saul Changes) 68
A Story for Today: The New Girl 71
Lighten Up: The Bully 76

CHAPTER 8: TALKING TO GOD 77

The Basics for Parents & Teachers 77
The Bible Story: Luke 6–11 (Jesus & Prayer) 78
A Story for Today: Prayer Changes Things 66
Lighten Up: The History Test .86

CHAPTER 9: CHURCH & MISSION 87

The Basics for Parents & Teachers 87
The Bible Story: John 15:9-17 (What Jesus Said) 88
A Story for Today: The Dance .92
Lighten Up: A Cup of Cold Water 96

IntRoDUCTIon

*If God is always with **me**, then how can God
be with other people too?*

Why do bad things happen to good people?

*Why should I pray if God
never answers my prayer the way **I** want?*

*Why did God send Jesus to earth if God knew
Jesus was going to die anyway?*

Every adult who has ever worked with children in the church setting
has encountered one of these questions at one time or another. This
kind of question stops you in your tracks and you haven't the foggiest
idea of how to answer. You know it's a serious question. You know you
should be able to answer it. But you don't know how to put your
thoughts into some kind of logical sentence that will make sense to a
child.

These questions and many more are addressed in this book. ***Building
a Heart of Faith*** gives parents and Sunday school teachers a
theological underpinning that will help them express complicated
theological concepts in a language even the younger boys and girls can
understand. An intergenerational study, this book doesn't avoid the
difficult topics but faces them head-on.

This book includes topics such as: God as the Creator who continues
to create, God as a spiritual presence in our lives, God as revealed
through Jesus, how the cross reveals the nature of God, God with us
in good times and in bad times, prayer as a special relationship with
God, how God transforms our lives from the inside out, and how we
are called to grow in love for God and one another.

HoW to USE tHiS BooK

Who is this book for?
This book is designed for parents, Sunday school teachers, and
children between the ages of 8 and 12 who want to have a better
theological understanding of God, of Jesus, and how the Bible calls
us to live.

When might you use it?

This book would be a good six-week study for adults and children during Lent or some other time when the whole church would like to focus on a common topic. There are times when everyone meets together; there will be times when groups meet in age level divisions.

How do you set up a group study?

Begin with the thought that much theology tends to be organized in a Trinitarian manner. While this book does not use the term, "Trinity," it does talk in this three-fold way of how we experience God.

1. a theology of God (Chapters 1–2),
2. a theology of Jesus Christ (Chapters 3–5),
3. and a theology of the Holy Spirit at work in our lives (Chapters 6–9).

A plan for a session together:

1. Bring everyone together in one place to hear the Bible story.

2. Divide into age-level groups to address the "Talking Together" questions.

   Adult Group: Read the Apostles' Creed together. Like the creed, many theologies begin with God, then move to consider God in Christ, and conclude with the Spirit, who empowers Christian living through the church.

   Children's Group: Use the "Talking Together" questions and some of the activities from the "Activity Corner" to make the session topic as concrete as possible.

3. Share "A Story for Today" in both groups separately. (Or you can bring both groups back together to hear this story and the discussion questions that follow.) Invite persons in both groups to share stories from their own lives that might relate. Use the discussion questions as jumping off points.

4. Send "Lighten Up" home with parents and children for further discussion.

creation

CHAPTER 1

WHAT WE WANT KIDS TO KNOW:

- **God is continually creating.**
- **God creates with the world, not on the world.**
- **God creates through loving, persuasive power.**
- **God creates by calling the world toward the good.**

THE BASICS FOR PARENTS & TEACHERS

Children encounter various stories of how our universe began. In addition to the Bible story that says that God created the universe, children also visit museums and see giant skeletons and hear stories of life in prehistoric times. The Creation story in Genesis 1 is a story of origins – one of several in the Bible. It does not necessarily conflict with the long era of the dinosaurs. Its writers, after all, had no notion of what we today call "science." Genesis simply tells us THAT God creates; the sciences lead us into an understanding of how our amazing universe is put together, or HOW God creates. Through our faith we believe God is deeply involved in creation. Scientific discoveries only increase our awe and wonder at the complexities of this universe. We don't want children to be afraid of scientific knowledge or feel that accepting science threatens their ability to have faith in God. Rather, we can teach them to begin with enthusiasm the lifelong process of combining faith and reason without violating either one.

The Bible begins with an account of God calling to the world and the world responding. God called the waters to separate, but it is the waters themselves that actually divided. God called land to appear, and it did; God called for vegetation, and the earth responded with plants. God told the first man and woman to be fruitful and multiply, but it was up to these human beings to actually do this. All of this responsiveness suggests the idea of a God who persuasively and lovingly called the world then toward new possibilities, increasing in complexity and goodness.

Children may be more familiar with the idea of a God who directly manipulates change in the world. These stories were part of the social language and understanding of our brothers and sisters from ancient days. Yet even among such stories, the Bible sews threads of God's constant love and nurturing guidance. As illustrated in the story "God's Call" (page 11), this nurturing guidance is in many ways more effective and more powerful than any forced manipulation.

Another point to be made is that the story of Creation is far from over. God's influence on the world did not stop after Genesis. By looking at the changes all around them, children can easily see that God is continually creating today.

So if God is continually calling the world into a new creation, what direction is God leading us toward? In our hearts, the answer is plain. God moves us toward new possibilities of goodness. God moves us toward a nurturing love with the goal of well-being for all. This movement toward goodness is portrayed in almost every verse of the Genesis story as God reacts to each part of Creation with the response, "God saw that it was good."

In the beginning, God created the heavens and the earth. The earth had no shape. Darkness covered the waters and everything else. The Spirit of God moved over the waters. Then God said, "Let there be light." And there WAS light! God saw that this light was good. Now there were both lightness and darkness. The lightness was called Day, and the darkness was called Night. And God liked this.

Then God said, "Let there be a dome in the middle of the waters." There was water on top and water on the bottom and a dome in the middle. The dome became the sky. And there was evening and morning, a second day.

Then God said, "Let the waters below the dome be gathered into one place, so that dry land might appear." And this happened. God called the dry land "earth," and the waters God called, "seas." God saw that this was good.

Then God said, "Let the earth start to grow things! Let there be plants, and fruit trees, with each kind having seeds so that there shall be more after them. And the earth did this: it brought forth all kinds of living plants and trees, and they all had seeds. And God saw that this was good. And there was evening and morning, a third day.

Then God said, "Let the sky be filled with stars and planets and moons. Let these celestial things separate our seasons and our months and our years. Let the sun give us light by day, and the rest give us light at night." And the sky did what God called it to do. And God saw that this was good. And there was evening and morning, a fourth day.

Then God said, "Let the waters produce all kinds of living creatures, and let there be birds to fly in all this sky." And the waters were filled with living creatures. The sky was filled with birds. God saw that all this was good. So God blessed all these creatures, telling them to have families. And there was evening and morning, a fifth day.

Then God said, "Let the earth produce living creatures: cattle and creeping things and beasts of the earth." And the earth was filled with animals, and all creatures big and small. They would all have families, and God saw that it was good.

Then God said, "Let us make people who are something like us, so that they can take care of all these things that we have made." And God created people, men and women, who could care for this wonderful earth. And God blessed them, and told them to have families. And God saw that all that had been made was good. And there was evening and there was morning, the sixth day.

On the seventh day, God rested and blessed that day and made it holy.

TALKING TOGETHER

1. Talk about how each thing that was created prepared the way for the next thing that was created.

2. Did God like this world and everything in it? How do you know?

3. What were people supposed to do?

4. Ordinarily a day means the time that it takes the earth to go around the sun one time. How long do you suppose a "day" in the Genesis story might be?

A STORY FOR TODAY   GOD'S CALL

Emily was creating a picture for part of a mural called "Creation." Her Sunday school teacher had told the class how wonderful it was that instead of just "zapping" things into existence, God had "called" everything to happen. Then it was up to whatever was called to do it. Emily's section of mural was under the words "Let there be light!" so the teacher had suggested she paint a big sun.

Emily had decided to paint a sky filled with stars instead. "Everybody knows that the sun is really a star," she told the two boys at her table. Secretly she hoped to impress them with this fact, but they didn't seem interested.

Emily looked up from her work and saw her older sister sneak past the classroom door. Emily wondered why her sister was in the hallway. She was supposed to be in her youth class.

"Mrs. Roberts," said Emily, "My sister's outside. I think she has a message for me. I'll be right back." Emily hurried out the door.

"Caitlin!" she called. "Wait! Where are you going?"

"Shhh!" Caitlin turned to her sister. "Why do you always have to ruin everything!"

Emily ran up to her so that she could speak more quietly. "But what are you doing in the hallway during Sunday school? I was worried that after your fight with Mom this morning you might be running away!"

Caitlin rolled her eyes. "Maybe I should. I can't believe Mom forces me to go to church! All I wanted to do was to go to Ashley's house instead of Sunday school. None of my friends have to go to church, so why do I?"

Emily had heard Caitlin and their mother arguing about this all

11

the way to church in the car. "If you're not running away, then where are you going?" she asked.

"Well, I WAS going across the street to Ashley's house. But now I can't 'cause you'll tell on me," said Caitlin.

"No I won't," said Emily, offended. "I've got an idea. I'll walk part of the way with you so people will think you're helping me with something."

Caitlin still seemed irritated, but she agreed to the plan. The two girls kept walking. Emily peeked into each room as they passed by.

"Look," said Emily. "They still have that big rocking horse in the nursery. Do you remember that? I loved that rocking horse."

"Actually, I do remember being in the nursery," said Caitlin. "I think."

In the next classroom they could see kids placing cookie dough onto baking sheets. "Oh, good," said Emily. "I bet the sixth graders are going to sell cookies before church."

The two girls had reached the door leading outside when they heard the choir beginning to practice. What a beautiful sound it was. Caitlin's hand was on the door knob, but she wasn't turning it. "I don't know why Mom thinks she can force me to go to church," she said again.

"That's right," agreed Emily. "You're in junior high. Church is for kids like me." She wondered why her sister wasn't opening the door. Meanwhile the harmonized voices from the choir room softly called. "So, when will you ...," began Emily.

"Maybe I shouldn't go to Ashley's," said Caitlin.

"OK," said Emily, a little surprised.

"But it's not because Mom and Dad are deciding for me!" Caitlin quickly added. "They are definitely not the boss of me!"

"No way! They can't tell you what to do," said Emily, looking up in admiration at her older sister.

Caitlin smiled back. "You know, if it wasn't for you maybe I would have gone to Ashley's house," she said. "Maybe God knows there are better ways of getting me to go to Sunday school than forcing me to do it." She ruffled Emily's hair, like she used to do when Emily was much younger.

"That's good, 'cause I need to finish my part of the mural," said Emily.

"Mural?" asked Caitlin. She put her hand on Emily's shoulder as they walked back to their respective classrooms.

"It's supposed to be a picture of God calling the light, so I drew stars," Emily explained. Caitlin raised her eyebrows as if Emily was crazy and then they both laughed together. "I'm glad you decided not to leave," said Emily.

The choir's singing reached a higher note. It was almost as if God was saying, "I'm glad too."

TALKING TOGETHER

1. What did Emily's teacher tell the class about God's creation?

2. Why do you think Caitlin didn't want to go to Sunday school and church?

3. How much force did God use to get Caitlin to change her mind?

4. How much do you think God forces you to do things?

5. Why do you think Caitlin decided to go back to Sunday school?

ACTIVITY CORNER

- Read the Creation story again. After each time God speaks with the sentence that begins "Let there be…" the group can dramatize the moment with some kind of predetermined noise. If possible, use a rhythm or musical instrument. Otherwise, have the children stomp their feet or drum on a table. Be creative. Point out how important God's call is in making our world a "good" creation.

- Collect leaves together, taking time to appreciate the beauty in the patterns and color of each one. Sort them according to size, shape and design. Use a magnifying glass to get "up close and personal."

- Use at least six different kinds of leaves. Put a roll of tape on the back of each leaf. Arrange them on a piece of paper. Overlap some of the leaves.

  Place a second piece of paper over the leaves. Remove the paper from old broken crayons. Lay each crayon on its side and rub it back and forth over the sheet of paper. Notice how the leaf pattern shows up on the second sheet of paper. Use more than one color.

  Talk about how God is continually creating, just as you have used the beautiful leaves to create another beautiful thing to appreciate.

GOD KEEPS CREATING!

GOD'S PRESENCE

CHAPTER 2

WHAT WE WANT KIDS TO KNOW:

- God's presence is not physical, but spiritual.
- We see God through the effects God has on the world.
- God is always working for the communal good.

THE BASICS FOR PARENTS & TEACHERS

Psalm 139 is the most beautiful expression in the Bible of the pervasive presence of God. The words of the Psalmist almost give a sense of playful delight, like some fanciful hide-and-seek game. "If I go to the heights, will I find you there? How about in the depths of the sea!" and always the answer is a delicious "yes! You are there!" It's like someone wrapping him or herself in a down comforter on a cold winter day. God surrounds us—behind us, before us, above us, beneath us, within us—there is nowhere without the presence of God. Perhaps we are so used to God's presence that we do not usually notice this wonderful reality. Then, sometimes, we become intensely aware of a presence that is always there, whether we feel it or not.

Small children are unusually open to a sense of God's reality. But they will try to visualize God physically rather than spiritually. That's appropriate for the age level. They can, however, begin to understand a surrounding, nurturing presence. As children mature toward the ages of 8 to 12, they commonly think of God through the image of light. This more closely matches the understanding that God's presence is not physical, but spiritual. As a spiritual presence, God exists pervasively and persuasively everywhere.

A person's image of God is very personal and should be respected even at the youngest age levels. For this reason it is best not to contradict a child's notion of how God appears, even if that notion is similar to a cartoon character. (After all, how many of us visualize God as the character from Michelangelo's Sistine Chapel painting?) Encouraging children to think about and explore how they see God will enhance and expand the idea of God in their lives.

There might be a need to discuss the ability of God to help more than one person simultaneously. Since God is always with us and always with other people too, God cannot be limited to any particular space.

Children can appreciate the fact that a concrete way to see God is through the effects God has on the world. When people listen to God's call rather than to destructive influences, results occur that lift others up, rather than bring them down. Unselfish acts such as spending time with a sick relative or having compassion for someone who doesn't fit in, are all like footprints of God in our world. By having God's loving presence in us, we can strive to love others in the same giving way.

In the story "The Footprint Hunt," Tyler's teacher gives the boys and girls the task of finding God in the church. Perhaps some of the children see a glimpse of God's wonder in the flowers, but when Tyler and Lucas help their injured friend, the children can see a true footprint of God. Seeing acts of compassion is a way of seeing God at work in the world.

Because God's presence is spiritual rather than physical, what *we* do physically matters tremendously. An old saying has it that "God has no hands but our hands." God calls us in *every* moment to work toward the communal good. Acting on this call can bring a sense of well-being to us as individuals, and can contribute to communities of well-being in the wider world. By doing so, we are intentionally living in God's presence.

The Bible has a section called Psalms. It is a book of 150 hymns and prayers and stories of what God's presence has meant to God's people. Psalm 139 was thought to be written by King David long, long ago. But its meaning is as true for us today as it was way back then. This Psalm is written not as a story, but as a prayer. Listen to the words. Think about it. Can you pray it too?

O Lord, you know everything about me, inside and out. You know when I sit down, and when I get up again. You even know what I am thinking about before I do myself! You see me when I go out, and when I lie down. You are familiar with every single thing I do. Before a word is on my tongue, you know exactly what I mean and what I am going to say!

You surround me—you are in front of me and behind me, and it's as if you laid a hand upon me in blessing. Such knowledge is too wonderful for me, almost more than I can even think!

Where can I go from your Spirit? Where could I ever get away from you? If could fly way up into the skies, you'd be there. If I go deep, deep under the earth, you'll be there! If I rise on the wings of the dawn, if I settle on the far side of the sea, even there your hand will guide me, your right hand will hold me fast!

If I say, "Surely the darkness will hide me, and the light become night around me," even the darkness will not be dark to you. The night will shine like the day, for to you darkness is the same as light.

You created my innermost being. You knit me together before I was even born. I praise you, for I am fearfully and wonderfully made, and your works are wonderful. I know that very well! When I was first turning into myself inside my mother's body, even then, you knew me. You could see my life before I'd ever lived it!

How precious to me are your thoughts, O God! How vast they are! If I should be able to count them, they would outnumber the grains of the sand. And when I wake up in the morning, I am still with you.

If only people who do bad things would turn from their wicked ways, and their wickedness be no more! I hate it when people seem to hate you, or rise up against you! They seem like my enemies, too! Oh, let me be an echo of your goodness! Search me, O God, and know my heart. Test me, and know my anxious thoughts. See if there is any offensive way in me, and lead me in the way everlasting.

TALKING TOGETHER

1. How do you think the writer felt when writing this Psalm?

2. How do you think the writer felt about God being like a surrounding presence all the time? Did he want to get away from this? How do you think he was feeling when he found God everywhere?

3. Is there any place where God isn't?

4. If God is with us all the time, do you think we get used to God's presence so much that we just don't notice it?

5. What things happen because God is present all the time?

6. In the very last part, the psalmist talks about God searching him, knowing him, testing him, and leading him. How do you suppose God does this?

THE FOOTPRINT HUNT

Tyler's new Sunday School teacher, Ms. White, was asking a lot of questions. All the girls in class had their hands raised up to answer. They kept their arms up even in between questions, just to make sure they had a turn to talk.

Lucas, Tyler's best friend, usually did very well at answering questions, but today he seemed interested in something else. He was looking up while rolling his head around at odd angles. Tyler felt bored and decided to raise his hand.

"Tyler," Ms. White called with a smile. "Where do you think we can find God?"

"In church," he said.

Emily smirked, "I already said church." Tyler felt embarrassed because he really hadn't been listening. He hoped Lucas would say something to support him, but Lucas was still looking up at the ceiling.

"Everyone seems to think that we can find God at church. So, there's only one thing to do," said Ms. White, "I'm going to give each group fifteen minutes to go around our building and find God. Then we'll all report back."

Lucas suddenly stopped looking upward. Ms. White paused thoughtfully before saying, "Lucas, were you searching for God up above us?"

"Nope, I was cracking my neck," he said simply.

Ms. White shook her head, as if disappointed by his answer, but then said, "The truth is, God can't be seen as easily as we see the regular, physical stuff in our world. That is because God is spiritual, which means God can be everywhere and in everything at the same time. One way we can see God, though, is to see the good things that God helps us to do. What we will look for today are these sort of God 'footprints.'" She went on to explain how everyone should choose a partner, be on their best behavior, and go look for God.

The two boys set off together and made their way to the donut table. Emily and April ran past them to get there first.

"Hey! It's not a race!" said Tyler as he jumped out of Emily's way. She looked back at him and made a face. It was while her head was turned that she tripped over her own feet and fell to the floor. No one made a sound. Tyler hoped Emily would not make a fuss. He had heard Emily cry before and it wasn't pretty. One moment later the air was filled with her whiney sobs. April looked very uncomfortable. Lucas was the first to say anything.

"Go get Emily a donut," he told April.

"I don't want a donut!" yelled Emily. "I want my Mom!"

"I'll go find her Mom," said April, and she quickly took off. Tyler wanted to run away too.

"I'll go find Ms. White," he said, heading back to the classroom. But when he got there, the classroom was empty. Everyone must still be out on the God Hunt. Tyler kept going down the hallway to the church's side yard. There by some rose bushes was Ms. White with other kids from his class.

"Do you see God in the flowers?" Tyler heard her say. How could she talk about flowers when Emily may have broken her leg?

"Ms. White!" he shouted. "Emily is hurt!"

Instantly Ms. White and the children headed towards him. As Tyler rushed them to the scene of the accident he described how loudly Emily had been screaming. "It sounded like she may have broken all kinds of bones!" he said.

But when they arrived to where Emily had fallen there was no crying at all. Emily and Lucas were sitting together on the ground, looking up at the sky.

You're right, Emily was saying. "It really does feel good." Lucas looked over at Ms. White.

"We're cracking our necks," he said.

"Yeah. It is so cool!" said Emily. "I scratched up my leg a little, but April went to get my Mom already."

"Thank goodness you're all right!" Ms. White said to Emily, but she made Emily get up and walk around just to make sure.

Then Ms. White gave a big smile to Lucas. "Class," she announced to everyone, "The help Lucas, Tyler and April have shown for their friend Emily is a true sign that God is here. It shows the goodness of helping others. Church is not the only place where we see how God helps us do good things, but we've found a definite footprint of God here today."

TALKING TOGETHER

1. Since we can't see God like we do other people, what is there about God that we **CAN** see?

2. How do you think people can see God in a flower?

3. How do you think people can see God in other people?

4. If helping Emily was a "footprint" of God, where else could God be at that moment?

5. What signs of God have you seen today?

ACTIVITY CORNER

- On a white piece of paper, use a white crayon to write the word "GOD." Make sure this is done firmly enough so that the letters can be felt. Paint on the paper with water colors and see how the God letters become clear.

  Talk about how the wax affected the water. Use this to explain how even though we can't see God with our eyes, we can see the effect of God in the world.

- Ask the child to describe what sort of picture comes to them when they think about God. If you have access to the Internet at church, go to the Google website and click on Images. Type in the word "God" and view the photos together. Some may be from other religions or cultures.

  No one can really know how God looks, since God is spiritual rather than physical. Ask if any photos remind the children of how **they** see God.

CHRISTMAS

CHAPTER 3

WHAT WE WANT KIDS TO KNOW:

- **Through Jesus we understand what God is like.**
- **God uses lowly things for wonderful purposes.**
- **Nothing is too small for God's attention.**

THE BASICS FOR PARENTS & TEACHERS

The Christmas story is so wonderful that we eagerly tell it to children. Nativity scenes in stores, on lawns, and in our living rooms show Jesus lying in a manger. Christmas cards and Christmas carols repeat the story: Jesus is Immanuel, God with us. We traditionally give gifts to one another on this day because it celebrates God's own gift to us—Jesus.

Christmas is a story of reversals, where expectations are disrupted by the breaking in of God's reign. This is consistent with the parables Jesus taught, for there, too, Jesus overturns the expectations of the listeners in order to give them a sense of the way God sees the world, and the way God calls us to be.

The "great reversal" of Luke's Christmas story is that "glory to God in the highest" is revealed within the roughness of a manger—a feed trough used for animals. The deepest splendor of Christmas is the paradox that God, the highest, becomes present to us in an unexpected place—in fact, the lowliest of places. Martin Luther called this the "mystery of the hidden God."

The theme of God as being present in the lowliest of places is repeated throughout Jesus' ministry, particularly in Matthew 25. There he tells his followers, "I was hungry and you gave me something to eat, I was thirsty and you gave me something to drink, I was a stranger and you invited me in, I needed clothes and you clothed me, I was sick and you looked after me, I was in prison and you came to visit me." When his followers ask, puzzled, "When did we do that?" Jesus responds, "I tell you the truth, whatever you did to one of the least of these, you did to me."

Christmas—God with us—wipes away the distinctions of value we make between "highest" and "lowest." Christmas tells us that no place is too lowly for the presence of God, and that God is to be found everywhere.

Christmas tells us that God gives the gift of Jesus to us, and that the love of God turns our world upside down, leading us to see value in unexpected places. It changes the way we see the world, for it means that against all our worldly standards and assumptions, God's glory can break out anywhere—perhaps where we least expect it.

Seeing the world in this way leads us to care about misery anywhere it is found. By caring and doing what we can to help, we are serving God. Shepherds paid honor to a baby so poor that his mother had no clothes for him, only cloths to wrap around him; no crib for his bed, but only a manger fit for feeding farm animals. But in paying honor to this one, they honored God's own self, hidden in a manger.

In those days Caesar Augustus wanted to know just how many people lived in his kingdom, so he sent out an order that all people living under Roman rule should be counted. This was called a census. People had to go to the town or city where they had been born, and register there so that they could be counted.

Joseph left his home in Nazareth, which was in the area called Galilee in the country of Judea—a very small part of the Roman Empire. He and his wife Mary, who was expecting a child, went to Bethlehem, where Joseph had been born. King David, who ruled over Israel in ancient times, had also been born in Bethlehem, and Joseph was one of David's descendants.

When Joseph and Mary arrived in Bethlehem to register, the time came for the baby to be born. But the town was full, and there had been no room for them at the inn, so they were staying that night in a stable. Mary gave birth to a baby boy. She wrapped him in cloths, and laid him in a manger, which was where they put hay for the animals to eat.

That very night there were shepherds living out in the fields nearby, keeping watch over their flocks of sheep. An angel of the Lord appeared to them, and the glory of the Lord shone around them.

The shepherds were terrified. They had never seen an angel before. But the angel said to them, "Don't be afraid. I bring you good news of great joy that will be for all people. Today in the town of David a Savior has been born to you. He is Christ, the Lord. This will be how you will know him: you will find him wrapped in cloths and lying in a manger."

Suddenly a great company of angels appeared with the first angel, and they were all praising God, and saying, "Glory to God in the highest, and on earth peace to those on whom God's favor rests!"

When the angels had gone away, the shepherds said to one another, "Let's go to Bethlehem and see this thing that the Lord has told us about."

The shepherds hurried off and found Mary, and Joseph, and the baby, who was lying in the manger just as the angel had said. When they had seen him, they spread the word among everyone they saw about what they had been told about this child. All who heard it were amazed.

Mary treasured all these things, thinking about them in her heart. The shepherds returned to the fields, glorifying and praising God for all the things they had heard and seen, which were just the way the angel had said.

TALKING TOGETHER

1. Have you ever seen a manger? What do you think a manger looks like? What is a manger used for?

2. What did the angels say was so special about the birth of this baby?

3. Sometimes we think palaces and mansions are where special people live. Jesus is the most special person ever born. Why do you suppose he wasn't born in a palace or a mansion?

4. The angels sang, "Glory to God in the highest," but the Christmas story tells about Jesus being born to people who had neither a home nor a place to stay in Bethlehem. Jesus was born in about the poorest place

possible. If God is in "the highest," but Jesus is in "the lowest," and if God is in Jesus, doesn't that seem topsy-turvy? If "the highest" is in "the lowest," is the "lowest" still low?

5. A song often sung at Christmas (Handel's The Messiah) quotes a verse from the Book of Isaiah in the Old Testament, saying, "Every valley shall be exalted, and every mountain and hill laid low." This means that "high" and "low" are turned upside down. Can you think how the birth of Jesus turns the way we value things upside down?

6. In Luke's Christmas story, it is shepherds whom God tells about Jesus. In Matthew's Christmas story, it is wise men, that tradition sometimes called kings, whom God tells about Jesus. The shepherds were poor, and the wise men were rich. Why do you suppose the message came to both?

LOVE CAME DOWN

The church was packed. The whole church had come to see the children's Sunday school Christmas program. Tyler yawned. He had been in these pageants practically since he was born. Mrs. Morris, the choir director, gave him a "look" and then motioned for all the kids to stand up straighter. They were about to begin the sixth song of the program.

"Love came down at Christmas," the group sang out. They were only a *little bit* behind the music on the CD. There was a microphone set up next to Mrs. Morris. That's where the children would stand to sing their solos. Tyler was grateful that his only job this year was to read a Bible verse at the end of the show. Austin, a kindergartner, was setting up to sing verse two all by himself.

"Stars and angels gave the sign." This was the signal that the first verse had ended. That was also when Austin fell over.

Something about the way he fell didn't look quite right. Mrs. Morris quickly turned off the music. The church was so quiet you could hear bulletins rustle.

Austin's mom came rushing to her son from the audience. Austin was beginning to turn green.

"He's going to throw up," whispered one of the girls anxiously. And sure enough, Austin did just that—all over the floor.

Two other women from the congregation came forward and were talking with Austin's mom in quiet voices. Then one of them rushed out of the sanctuary. The other spoke with Pastor Lynn. Long minutes were passing, and still the church was silent.

Finally Pastor Lynn stood up and said in a calm voice, "We're pretty confident that Austin is OK, but it's always good to take precautions. We've called medical professionals. While we wait for them, why don't we all pray and sing together."

Everyone got quiet once more. Pastor Lynn started the prayer. The prayer said something about the glory of Christmas being seen in how people helped each other in time of need or something.

Tyler had a hard time paying attention. *"How could Austin's falling over or throwing up have anything to do with Christmas?"* he wondered to himself.

"Now, let's sing hymn number 71," said the pastor.

None of the kids had hymnals. But the organist began to play a familiar carol, "Angels We Have Heard on High." Some of the kids around Tyler tried mumbling the words, but most were too busy staring at Austin who was now crying and hugging his mother tightly.

"Gloooooria," sang the congregation. Pastor Lynn walked right in front of the kids and playfully encouraged them to sing along with gusto. The girls picked up the tune, and sang louder and louder. "In excelsis Deo!" Tyler found himself joining in. Then somebody's dad passed a hymnal up to the choir. It was open to the right page. Soon other people offered their hymnals as well.

Tyler almost didn't notice that three paramedics had entered the sanctuary. They knelt down beside Austin and his mother. Everyone just kept singing and trying to see what was happening.

All of a sudden Mary, who was in kindergarten with Tyler's little sister, began to cry. Emily reached over and tried to comfort her, but the little girl wouldn't stop. Her cries got louder and louder. Her mother came to the front and led her back to where the family was sitting. The song ended.

Tyler thought that the pastor would bring the program to an end. But instead of stopping the program, Pastor Lynn stepped up to the microphone. "Life throws us many surprises including the kind experienced by Austin and his family today. But it's the love of God, seen here by the concern of our congregation and the care by the paramedics, that we can always count on to get us through. Christmas is all about that love. So let's conclude the Sunday school program about this wonderful gift."

At least," thought Tyler, "there's only one song left to sing." Just before the last verse, Emily stepped up to the microphone. This was her solo. Considering the ruckus that had just occurred, she sang it amazingly well. Tyler gave her a thumbs up as she returned to the group.

Then it was Tyler's turn. He took a piece of paper from his pocket and stepped up to the microphone. "Romans 8," Tyler could see his parents smiling proudly at him. "For I am convinced that neither death, nor life, nor angels, nor rulers, nor things present, nor things to come, nor powers, nor height, nor depth, nor anything else in all creation, will be able to separate us from the love of God in Christ Jesus our Lord."

And the whole congregation as one said, "Amen."

TALKING TOGETHER

1. What were some of your happiest Christmas times? What were you doing? Who else was involved?

2. What do you like the most about Christmas presents? What is your favorite Christmas present of all times?

3. What kind of presents don't come in a box?

4. How is God's love like a present?

5. How is God's love different and better than a present in a box?

6. How do you think love stays the same size?

- Using a Nativity Creche, retell the Christmas story with the children. Ask: "What comes next?" as each piece is played out. Use the pieces to guide their telling of the story rather than doing it for them. Point out how unusual it was to have shepherds visited by angels and Jesus, the son of God, born as a poor baby.

- Make Christmas cards together, using crayons, stickers or markers to make a picture on the front of the card. At the beginning of the inside of the card, help or have the children write "Dear ____" to whatever person they are going to send the card. At the bottom of the card write "Love," and the child's name. Ask them what words or images remind them of Christmas. Talk about how the most important part of the card is making someone else feel loved and happy, like we do with the spirit of Christmas.

- If you have a lighted Christmas tree at your home, gather the family together, sitting on the floor. Put on a favorite Christmas CD. Turn off all the lights except for those on the tree. Think about how lovely and peaceful this moment is.

STORiES JESUS TOLD

WHAT WE WANT KIDS TO KNOW:

- A parable is a short story that illustrates a point.

- Jesus used parables to teach us how God sees the world.

- Through parables, Jesus showed us about the radical love of God.

THE BASICS FOR PARENTS & TEACHERS

In the gospels of Matthew, Mark, and Luke, Jesus' teaching ministry is marked by stories we call "parables." A parable is a brief story that forcefully illustrates a single idea, usually a comparison of some kind. Jesus used these stories to teach about God and God's kingdom.

Most parables begin with a familiar situation (i.e. two men going up to the temple to pray, one a religious Pharisee, the other a despised tax collector). Jesus' audience would *anticipate* an ending that praises the Pharisee. But instead, Jesus' parables turned things upside down. In this particular story, Jesus lifts up the importance of the tax collector's prayer.

Again and again the parables upset common assumptions about the way things **should** be, surprising the hearers by reversing their expectations, causing them to re-evaluate their views. The parable we've selected for our Bible story in this chapter does this by making the Samaritan the one who does **good.**

In Bible times, Samaritans were considered anything **but** good. Because "Good Samaritan" has entered our language as an admirable term, we have lost some of the original power of the parable. To Jesus' hearers, a Samaritan was a person who did not follow the law and worship of the Hebrews. There was ill-feeling between the Samaritans and the Jews in New Testament times. So this story announced a different way of creating a community of well-being in which all are valued.

You might be able to help the children understand this by replacing the words "priest," "Levite," and "Samaritan" with words from their own experience. (Note: Remember to make the Samaritan someone whom you would least expect to offer compassion and help.)

Jesus' parables serve as examples of the kind of conduct God expects of us. But the point of the parables is never simply to tell us how to act or live. The focal point of all the parables is to announce the coming of God's reign. In God's kingdom, ordinary expectations and values are turned upside-down, replaced by God's values. God abolishes our usual distinctions of worth and establishes God's universal love. The "peace on earth" announced by the angels at Christmas becomes exemplified in Jesus' teaching.

It is far easier to tell these parables to children as "example" stories, telling us how to live. But it is also important to give some sense as well about the original meaning of the parables, the announcement of what God's kingdom should be like.

Once while Jesus was speaking to a group of people, a man who knew the laws of Israel quite well stood up. He wanted to see if Jesus could answer a hard question. "Teacher," he asked, "what should I do to inherit eternal life?"

"What is written in the Law?" Jesus answered. "How do you understand it?"

The man answered, "Love the Lord your God with all your heart and with all your soul and with all your strength and with all your mind, and also, love your neighbor as yourself."

"That's a very good answer," said Jesus. "Do this, and you will have eternal life."

But the man wanted to show that he knew what he was talking about, so he asked Jesus a question: "Who is my neighbor?"

Jesus answered him by telling this story:
A man was going down from Jerusalem to Jericho, walking a long way, when suddenly he was attacked by robbers. The robbers took his money and his clothes, beat him up until they nearly killed him. Then they went away, leaving the man half dead by the side of the road.

Some time later a priest happened to be going down the same road. When he saw the man, he quickly walked to the other side of the road and passed him by. Later on another man who worked in the temple came to that same place. When he saw the man, he too passed by on the other side.

Then a Samaritan came down the road. Nobody in that country liked Samaritans very much. They thought Samaritans should stay where they belonged in their own country, and not come into Israel at all. Samaritans worshiped God in a strange way.

A Samaritan certainly wouldn't do anything to help someone. But this Samaritan felt sorry for the injured man.

The Samaritan went to him, put healing ointment on his wounds, and then bandaged him. The Samaritan lifted the man onto his own donkey, and led him down the road until he came to an inn. There the Samaritan took a room, and watched over the man all night.

The next day before he left, the Samaritan gave the innkeeper some money. "Take care of this man. If it costs you more than this, I will pay you when when I come back this way."

When Jesus finished the story, he turned to the man who had asked him the question, "Which of these three people do you think was a neighbor to the man who had been injured?"

"Well," said the man, "The one who took pity on him."

"Now, you go and do the same thing," said Jesus.

1. What would the story sound like if instead of the word "priest" you said "minister," and instead of the words for the "other person who worked in the temple" you said "Sunday school teacher," and instead of saying "Samaritan" you said "illegal alien," or the name of a person from some other group who isn't much liked in your community?

2. If the story said that a man had been beaten and robbed and left by the side of the road, and the next part of the story said that a minister came by, what would you think the story would say next? Why would you be surprised that the minister didn't do what you expected?

3. What would you expect the second religious person to do?

4. Why do you suppose Jesus made the good guy in the story be someone most people would not like?

5. If you were one of the people listening to Jesus, do you think it would change the way you thought about Samaritans from that time on?

6. Could this story change the way we think about groups of people that lots of folks don't approve of?

7. Jesus shows us what God is like, and what God wants us to be like. Sometimes we call this "the reign of God."

A STORY FOR TODAY

THE VISITORS

Three boys were visiting Tyler's Sunday school class. They were part of a group that had come in a bus from a downtown church. It didn't look like the boys were blending in well with the other kids. Tyler was a little afraid of them. They talked loudly among themselves in a way that seemed different and rough. Unfortunately, the Sunday school teacher that morning was having a very boring lesson.

"What I would like for you to learn today," she said, after making everyone sit down on the floor and look at her, "is how Jesus changed the social rules of his time. Jesus wanted everyone to be welcome in church, not just the rich MEN."

Tyler and his friend Lucas were sitting near one of the boys from the visiting church. He was looking more and more bored as the teacher talked on about how important it was for everyone to accept others, just like Jesus did. Then the boy interrupted to say, "I have to go to the bathroom." There was silence as the teacher thought this over. All the kids knew this was the oldest trick in the book to get out of a boring class.

"Do you know where the bathroom is?" the teacher asked.

"I'll show him," said Lucas.

"Why does Lucas have to be so brave?" Tyler thought to himself. *"That means I have to be brave too."*

"I'll go too!" Tyler said out loud and the teacher nodded at them both. She kept on talking as the three boys left the class.

"My name is Lucas," said Lucas, "He's Tyler." They walked down the hallway.

"I'm Raymond," said the boy.

Then Lucas began to chatter about how lucky it was that the teacher had let them all leave the class together.

"Last week we video taped the story of Moses," said Tyler, trying to let Raymond know that the class was usually more "cool" than today.

"My Dad used to be in a gang," said Raymond.

Tyler wasn't quite sure what else to say. Was Raymond trying to shock them?

"My sister got picked up for shoplifting," said Lucas.

"What!" gasped Tyler turning to stare at Lucas. He had always looked up to Lucas's older sister. Why would she would ever do such a thing?

"That's not a good thing," said Raymond as he shook his head.

"Your sister **steals** stuff?" asked Tyler with disbelief.

"She had already spent her allowance and she really wanted the hair clip," said Lucas.

Just then, a man from the visiting church appeared from out of nowhere. "What are you boys doing?" he asked sternly. Tyler's face turned red.

"We were just showing Raymond to the bathroom," he stammered.

"This boy's sister steals!" said Raymond.

"And Raymond was telling us how it's not a good thing," added Lucas quickly.

"You got that right!" said the man. "It's just like I told you, Raymond. This church is not as different as you think. They have some of the same problems we have in our community."

"Wow," gasped Tyler, once they were alone again. "I thought for sure we were going to be in trouble! Who is that man anyway?"

"Mr. Jackson. He's my Sunday school teacher and he's cool," said Raymond. Then he smiled—the first real one

Tyler had seen on his face. "He's not nearly as boring as your teacher!"

Tyler suddenly felt as if the three of them had a lot more in common than they thought. "Well, she's usually not this bad. Let us tell you about the movie we made about Moses last week." Then the three hurried on down the hallway to the bathroom before anyone got suspicious and came looking.

TALKING TOGETHER

1. What makes you afraid of other people?

2. Why do you think Tyler was afraid of Raymond at first?

3. Do you think Raymond may have felt uncomfortable at Tyler's church?

4. What made Tyler feel more comfortable?

5. What are some things that are the same for everybody, no matter where they are from?

6. Which people do you think God cares the most about?

7. Who do you think God wants us to care about?

ACTIVITY CORNER

- Fill a glass bottle to the very top with water. Place an index card on top of the bottle. Holding the card in place, turn the bottle upside down. Ask your child to predict what will happen when you take your hand away from the card. Although it might be expected that the water will gush out, show how the weight of air pushing all around us (14 pounds for every square inch) holds up the card and keeps the water in the bottle. Talk about how stories that Jesus told often turned what people expected should happen upside down.

- In Jesus' time, persons assumed that foreigners, women, children, and persons with diseases weren't as important as other persons in the community. But Jesus told stories that explained that all persons are important. Have the children name five people that they think are important. Draw their portraits. Make a gallery of important people.

- Look at the pictures here. Can you tell what they are? Turn the page upside down and read the answers. The stories Jesus told often opened people's eyes to a new way of seeing things, too. Instead of only thinking selfishly, Jesus wanted everyone to treat each other with kindness. This way of living is how we describe the Kingdom of God on earth.

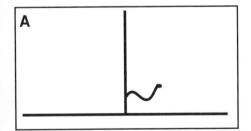

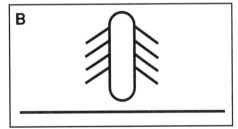

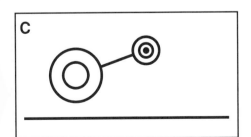

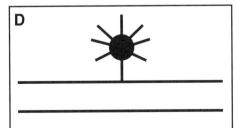

a. a cat with its tail caught in an elevator door; b. a fish-eye view of a rowing team; c. a person in a big hat frying an egg; d. a spider doing a handstand.

45

46

GOOD FRIDAY & EASTER

CHAPTER 5

WHAT WE WANT KIDS TO KNOW:

- **God is progressively revealed to us in Jesus.**
- **This revelation comes to a conclusion on Good Friday and Easter.**
- **We learn that God is the power of resurrection.**

THE BASICS FOR PARENTS & TEACHERS

Christmas, Good Friday and Easter are the heart of the Christian faith. These events, along with the teachings of Jesus, reveal the love of God to us. It's easy for children to hear stories about Christmas, and about the teachings of Jesus, but it's not so easy to talk about Good Friday and the crucifixion. But unless we have some understanding of why there is a Good Friday, then we can't make sense of Christmas and Easter.

The cross of Jesus can be understood in several ways:

Jesus' death is a ransom for our sins. This particular view is depicted in C.S. Lewis' *The Lion, The Witch, and the Wardrobe*, which many children know. When Adam sinned, he and all his descendants automatically became servants of Satan. Only by "ransoming" us from Satan could we be saved from death. God (through Jesus) offers to die instead of us, and we are made free. God being who God is, death cannot hold him.

Jesus' death provides payment for our sins. If someone unjustly offends another person, the offender offers to pay "satisfaction" to the offended party. The satisfaction had to be something equal to the offense. When human beings sin, we offend God. Only an *infinite* payment can wipe out the offense. Human beings cannot make such a payment. Therefore, God through Jesus, dies; his death meets the criteria for satisfaction. Through faith in Christ, our debt is paid in full.

Justification by faith. In Adam we have all violated the law of God. We deserve to be punished. The punishment for sin is death. By Jesus' death on the cross, Jesus receives the punishment we deserve. Because Jesus does not deserve this punishment, God raises him. Through our belief in Jesus, we are pardoned for our violations. John Wesley understood Christ's death for our sin as satisfying the justice of God. The reason Christ dies for our sin is grounded in God's everlasting nature, which is love.

The cross reveals of the nature of God. Jesus' birth, life, death, and resurrection are a revelation of the nature of God. Through Jesus' teachings we are called to participate in God's generous love toward the world, working toward the well-being of all. The death of Jesus reveals that God experiences our sins, so that the harm we do to one another is done to God as well. The resurrection of Jesus reveals God's power to transform our hatred to love, our sins to acts of mercy, our deaths to life. God is the resurrection power of the universe.

No matter which of the above understandings reflect our beliefs, it is essential that we all understand the interrelatedness of Good Friday and Easter, the cross and the Resurrection. In Good Friday we see God's resurrection power—a power to continue to love even in the deepest pain. The resurrection on Easter morning is the culmination of the revelation of God that began with Jesus' birth, continued in the message Jesus taught, and was manifested in his crucifixion.

After finishing supper with his disciples, Jesus told them that "God would be in them," just as God was always in Jesus. He knew that terrible things were about to happen, and he prayed that God would strengthen the disciples, so that they would be loving people. Then Jesus prayed for everyone like us, who live a long time after this story. He prayed that we would know that God loves us just as God loves Jesus. He prayed that we would be a part of God's love, too.

After dinner, Jesus and his disciples went across the valley to an olive grove to pray. Judas knew they would be there, and he brought the soldiers with him to arrest Jesus.

The soldiers arrested Jesus and brought him to the high priest, who questioned him. "I have always spoken openly," said Jesus, "Why are you questioning me? Ask the people who heard me."

Jesus' answer angered one official so much that he hit Jesus. Jesus looked at the man, "I spoke the truth. Why did you hit me?"

The high priest then sent Jesus to Pilate, the Roman governor. Only the Romans could sentence a person to die. But Pilate could find nothing that Jesus had done wrong. He wanted to release him, but the group of people who brought Jesus there said, "No."

By this time a crowd of people had gathered outside. During festival days, it was customary to release a prisoner. Pilate offered the people a choice—He could release Barabbas, a known criminal or Jesus. The crowd chose Barabbas. So Pilate did as they asked.

The soldiers made fun of Jesus. People had called Jesus King of the Jews," so they put a crown of thorns on his head and a purple robe around his shoulders. Then Pilate presented Jesus to the crowd once again, asking what should happen to him. "Crucify him!" the crowd shouted. And once again Pilate did as they asked.

Jesus was forced to carry his cross through the city streets to a place just outside the city gate. Here the soldiers crucified Jesus, between two criminals. Above Jesus' head, the soldiers attach a wooden sign: Jesus of Nazareth, the King of the Jews. Later that evening, Jesus died. His last words were, "It is finished."

A man named Joseph, from a place called Arimathea, asked Pilate for the body of Jesus. Then he and Nicodemus, prepared Jesus' body for burial and laid it in a garden tomb. The two men rolled a great stone in front of the door. Then they left, for it was the sabbath.

Early on the first day of the week, while it was still dark, Mary Magdalene went to the tomb. She saw that the stone had been rolled away from the entrance and ran to find Simon Peter and the other disciples. Jesus' body was not in the tomb!

Peter and another ran to the tomb. Inside, they found strips of the linen burial cloths, but no Jesus. Neither could understand what had happened, so they left. Meanwhile, Mary Magdalene stood outside the tomb, crying. When she bent to look inside the tomb, she saw two angels where Jesus' body had been!

"Why are you crying?" the angels asked her.

"They have taken away my Lord," she said, "and I don't know where they have put him."

Mary turned around and saw a man standing there. She thought it must be the gardener or caretaker. The man asked, "Woman, why are you crying? Who are you looking for?"

Not looking up, Mary said, "Sir, if you have taken him away, please tell me where you have put him, and I will get him."

Then Jesus called her name and she recognized his voice. "Teacher!" she cried.

Jesus said, "Go to my disciples and tell them that I am returning to my father and your father, to my God and your God."

Mary Magdalene ran to where the disciples were staying. "I have seen the Lord!" she told them and she repeated what he had said.

That evening the disciples gathered together inside a locked room. They were afraid. They did not understand what was happening. Suddenly Jesus was there in the room with them.

"Peace be with you!" Jesus said. He showed them his wounds to prove that he was indeed Jesus. The disciples were no longer afraid, but overjoyed. Jesus was alive!

TALKING TOGETHER

1. What did Jesus pray for at the beginning of this story?

2. Do you ever wonder why anyone would want to hurt Jesus? Sometimes people do things that hurt other people. This is called sin. It was sin to put Jesus on the cross. Would it be a sin to put anyone on a cross? Why?

3. Sometimes when we are hurting inside, we think that God must be far away. Do you think God was far away from Jesus on the cross? What makes you think that God was still with Jesus?

4. What do you think it means that God is with us, even when we are hurting and don't feel God in any way?

5. The only thing that makes the day Jesus died "Good Friday" is because of what happened on that first Easter morning. Even today, we sing glad and happy songs on every Easter. Tell the Easter part of the story!

6. Think about how Jesus' story becomes a part of our story, too. By hearing about God through Jesus, and letting what we hear influence the way we live, we are Christians. Being a Christian means knowing God through Jesus, and letting God's love shape the way we love.

A STORY FOR TODAY

BUILDING UP

It was a hot summer day, too hot. Tyler had hoped that his mom would take him and his friend Lucas to the beach. Instead they were stuck at the church playground while she attended some emergency church meeting about tablecloths or something. He and Lucas half-heartedly swung on the swings, letting their feet drag along the sandy ground.

"Hey," said a familiar voice. It was their friend Emily. She was with a boy that neither of the boys recognized.

"This is my cousin, Kyle," she explained. "He's visiting from Kansas, but mom brought us here 'cause she has a dumb meeting today."

Lucas looked at Kyle with interest.

"Kansas, huh? Do you live near Dodge City?" he asked.

Kyle made a face. "Are you crazy?" he said, not very kindly. "What do you think I am, some kind of cowboy or something?"

"No," said Lucas, who was always very direct and did not take offense easily. "I did a report in school on Dodge City last year. I think it sounds like a cool place."

"Why, do you want to be a cowboy? Play shoot 'em up?" teased Kyle. Kyle made it clear what he thought about Lucas by the look on his face.

"Quit it, Kyle," said Emily, feeling a little embarrassed by her cousin's behavior.

But Kyle didn't seem like he wanted to quit. "Blam! Blam!" he went, pretending his fingers were six guns.

"*What a jerk,*" thought Tyler. "Yeah, real scary," he said out loud.

"Oh, yeah?" Kyle said angrily. "How about this!" Instead of using his finger guns, as he said "Blam! Blam!", he reached down and took a fistful of sand. He threw it directly at Tyler and Lucas.

"Hey!" shouted Tyler. Then without thinking, he grabbed sand and threw it right back at Kyle.

Soon sand was flying everywhere. Tyler was afraid to open his eyes, so he just kept picking up sand and throwing it in the direction of Kyle's laughter.

This went on for a couple of minutes. Then all of a sudden Tyler felt a cold blast of water spraying his chest.

"Stop it! Right now! I mean it!" Emily was shouting.

Tyler opened his eyes. There was Emily holding a garden hose. She was yelling at Kyle. "Just because your brothers tease and throw sand at you doesn't mean you have to do the same thing to other people!" she yelled. "Mom said we should be nice to you because of what's going on in your family. But I am NOT going to let you make me miserable too!"

At that moment, Pastor Linda came out onto the playground. "My goodness, children. I hate to intrude, but from my window I could see you making quite a ruckus over here." At this point Emily had burst into tears. Kyle was silent. Lucas knelt down in the sand. "You don't have to tell me exactly what was going on, but I think you should remember where you are. This is a church yard. Churches are places where we should be reminded of God's love.

At church we build each other up, not tear each other down."

The four kids didn't say anything at that point. They couldn't even look at each other. "Now, are you four OK on your own, or did you want me to see if your mothers can take you home?"

Emily stopped crying and shook her head. "We're OK, Pastor Linda, thanks," she said.

"Yeah, we're OK now," echoed Tyler.

The pastor smiled and went back to her office.

"Sorry I got you in trouble," said Kyle after she was out of earshot. He honestly looked like he was sorry.

Meanwhile, Lucas was still down on the ground. But now he was patting a clump of wet sand together. "Look," he said. "We could build stuff, just like at the beach."

The hose was still on, making a good supply of wet sand. Tyler noticed some buckets and play shovels next to the swings.

By the time the meeting at church was over with, Emily, Lucas, Tyler and Kyle had built a city of sand castles.

"Look at that," Emily's mom said to Tyler's mom. "What a creative thing to do with sand!" Tyler couldn't help smiling as he remembered how that very same sand had been used just about an hour earlier.

TALKING TOGETHER

1. Why do you think Kyle created such a "ruckus"?

2. What did Pastor Linda say that the church was?

3. What do these things tell us about God and Jesus?

4. How did the children turn something that was destructive into something constructive?

ACTIVITY CORNER

- Find pictures of how artists have drawn the crucifixion. Look at them together. Talk about how they make you feel. Explain how crosses were used in Bible times to punish and scare people from breaking the law. Show a piece of jewelry that uses a cross. Talk about how God helped change an ugly, scary thing into a symbol that is used to make beautiful jewelry. God can take any situation, no matter how bad, and help transform it into its best possible outcome.

- Show children how hymns in a hymn book are arranged in the order of church holidays. Find the Easter section and read through some of the hymns together. Look for verses that describe God and Jesus changing sadness into happiness.

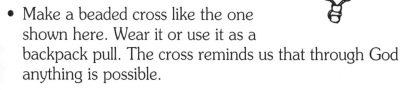

- Make a beaded cross like the one shown here. Wear it or use it as a backpack pull. The cross reminds us that through God anything is possible.

GOOD TIMES & BAD

CHAPTER 6

- **We live in a world where we are affected by many things, good and bad.**
- **God is with us in the bad times and the good times.**
- **God encourages us to live creatively even though bad things happen.**

THE BASICS FOR PARENTS & TEACHERS

Until faced with an actual traumatic event, most young children believe they live in a secure, well-ordered place. They believe that bad things are not going to happen or that all bad things are reversible. God's job, they assume, is to protect them from any harm. When a child encounters a tragedy, his or her sense of order is lost and fears develop for his or her own safety. The child begins to ask questions such as: Why did God allow this terrible thing to happen? This is even more intensified if the child had prayed for this event not to occur, such as the death of a loved one.

In previous chapters we discussed the nature of God's power. Rather than forcibly controlling our lives and our environment, God nurtures and guides us to move towards decisions and actions that provide the most good for all. This takes place in the midst of many, many other influences upon us – influences from our personal past, our social/cultural context, world political events, and natural things like the weather and illness. Because we live in a world where we are affected by many things, focusing on God's guidance towards the best of all possibilities is essential. A more appropriate question to ask when bad things happen should be: Lord, where is your path for me from this bad place?

Another aspect of multiple influences other than God is that it allows risk, which gives us appreciation for goodness, not to mention breath-taking adventures. Trying to live without risk or wants would make life very uninteresting and dull. This is illustrated in the contemporary story of Tyler's bird, which is included in this chapter. As Tyler's teacher says, the bird would prefer a life of exploring boundless horizons, even if some of those horizons may be dangerous.

The concept of God's call toward the ideal of universal well-being is not easily understood by children. But the children should find comfort in the knowledge that God is with us always. God is with us in the bad times. God is with us in the good times. God is with us even when we don't pay any attention to what God wants us to do.

We can see this theme in the familiar Bible story that we call "The Prodigal Son." (Actually, it is more the story of the "Forgiving Father.") A father allows his son to choose to leave home with his inheritance. The father, in his wisdom, knows that this is a very bad idea. But still he gives his son the freedom to make the choice. Unsurprisingly, things do indeed start going wrong.

Rather than blaming the father, however, the son realistically blames himself for his own poor choices. Beneath it all, however, the young man relies on the knowledge that his father continues to be there for him with a love that yearns for his homecoming. The son probably does not understand the full extent of his father's love, but he has enough trust to move away from his poor choices toward the good that his father might still provide for him.

We can assure children that God is not a powerless observer. God is right there with us. God's presence can strengthen us and guide us toward whatever positive steps can help move us out of suffering. We experience God's presence in a variety of ways. Sometimes it is quiet nudges toward the good; sometimes it is alertness to the possibilities of good;

sometimes it is a power for courage or compassion. In such ways, God encourages us to live creatively even though bad things happen.

We live in a world where we are affected by many things, bad and good. As impermanent as our world may be, the one permanence we can depend on is God. Even when bad things happen, God continues to call us to live creatively towards a better world for all.

THE BIBLE STORY

Luke 15: 11-32: THE PRODIGAL SON

A certain man had two sons. One day the younger one said to his father, "Father, give me my share of the family fortune, for I want to go off on my own and see the world." So the father divided his money between his two sons. Soon after this, the younger son gathered all his things together, and left home to go live in another place that was far away.

When the younger son got to the new place where he planned to live, he began to spend all his money. He had many friends, and they helped him spend his money. Life was fun and exciting. The younger son liked his new life.

Then a very bad thing happened in this new country. There was no rainfall that spring, and none of the crops grew well. Food became scarce and very expensive.

The young man had spent all his money and couldn't afford food. His new friends would not help him and so they disappeared. Jobs were also hard to find.

Finally, the younger son was able to find work taking care of pigs. Being very hungry, the young man soon began to eat the leftovers from the food he was giving to the pigs.

The young man started to feel very sorry for himself. He thought of his father's fine home. He thought of the good food he had had to eat there. He even thought about the people who worked for his father and how they even had good bread to eat, and places to sleep.

"I will go home," he said to himself. "Even though I have wasted everything my father gave me, and don't deserve a home there any more, I will ask father if I can work for him as a hired hand!" So the younger son started for home.

The young man thought that his father would surely have forgotten all about him. But what he did not know was that every day his father would walk down the road in front of their house, hoping to see his son coming home again. Each day the father turned back, disappointed. But on this particular day, the father saw his younger son coming down the road! His heart was filled with joy. He ran to his son, hugged him.

The son was crying. "Father, I've done so wrong. I don't deserve to be called your son any more."

Before he could ask his father for a job as a hired hand, his father shouted to the servants, "Quickly, bring out good clothes and shoes. Dress my son, and put this ring on his finger! Then let's have a big celebration! For my son, who was lost to me, has come back! I was afraid he had died, and instead, he's alive, and home safely!"

As the servants began preparing the party, the older son returned home from his work and saw what was happening. When he asked a servant what was going on, the servant said, "Your brother has come home! Your father is having a party!"

This made the older son angry. "Why should his brother have a party, after all he'd done?" he thought to himself.

Just then the father came into the room. He saw the older

son's face and knew exactly what his son was thinking. "All these years I've served you well. I've done everything you asked me to do, but when did you ever give *me* a party? This good-for-nothing brother of mine comes back after wasting everything you gave him, and you celebrate!"

His father hugged him and said, "My dear son, you have always been with me. All that I have is yours! But it's as if this brother of yours had been dead! And now he is alive again! He was lost! But now he is found! So instead of being angry, let's rejoice."

TALKING TOGETHER

1. What kinds of things went wrong for the father?

2. What kind of things could ever go wrong for God?

3. What are some of the reasons why things went wrong for the son?

4. Why should the older brother have welcomed the returning son instead of wanting him punished?

5. Is God more like the father or more like the older brother?

6. Do you think it would be wrong for the son to blame his father for his problems? Why?

7. Why do you think it is not right to blame God when things go wrong?

Tyler's loved Miss Jones, one of his Sunday school teachers. Not only was she beautiful, but she even sounded beautiful. She spoke with an English accent. Whenever she spoke, the whole class just gazed up at her.

Today Miss Jones was telling the class something about God and how the different things in the world influenced what people did. Tyler loved the way she pronounced "wahrld" Then she handed out butterfly nets to each of them and led them outside to catch some "interesting bugs."

"Isn't Miss Jones pretty?" whispered April as they headed outside with their nets. "I wished I looked like her."

Just then Lucas poked him and said, "I couldn't understand what she was saying. Now that we're out here, what are we supposed to do?"

"We're supposed to catch bugs," said Emily, "but I don't know what sort of bugs she expects us to find out here. Ants, maybe?"

Tyler drifted off from the others. He wanted to catch the most impressive bug he could find. Suddenly, he saw the bushes move—just slightly. There between the roots of a tree was a little gray bird. It looked confused and not very strong.

Tyler froze in place so as not to frighten it away. Then slowly he raised his butterfly net and lowered it with a "whoosh." The net trapped the little bird.

"I caught something! I caught something!" he yelled.

Lucas was the first to run over."Hey, it's a baby bird. Is it hurt?" he asked, crouching down to take a better look.

April was the next closest and came to take a look."Wow! A

bird!" she said. Soon everyone was gathered around. Miss Jones finally stepped into the circle to see what was happening.

"What do you think?" asked Tyler proudly.

"Oh, dear me, what do I think?" Miss Jones said as the little bird hopped against the netting, trying to escape.

Emily had left the circle and had gone to get a big box. "Let's put it in here, Tyler," she said. "It can be our class pet! We can get a real cage later."

"Hold on, Emily," said Miss Jones kindly. "Let's talk about this for a minute. Do we really need a class pet? What would be better for the bird?"

Emily set the box on the ground next to the net. "That's easy," she said. "If we take care of the bird, we can make sure it has a long life. It will never have to look for food and it will be safe from all kinds of things. Did you know that half the birds in the wild die the first year?"

"That's not true! It can't be" said Lucas. "Look at all the birds!"

Emily rolled her eyes and gave him an impatient look. "Yes it is. My Dad's a biology teacher. He knows all about stuff like that," she explained as if that statement alone would end the argument.

"But our science newsletter said that many birds live five years!" said Lucas.

Doubt crept over Emily's face for a moment, then she answered quickly, "I'm approximating."

"Boys and girls, please!" said Miss Jones. "What we have here is exactly what I was trying to explain in class. If God had **complete** control over our world, it would rather be like living in a box or a cage for us. Yes, we'd be safe and have everything we needed, but think how uninteresting it would be! I much prefer having a world around me with lots of influences, not life in a box. That way we have endless possibilities, not just one. Think of all the new horizons to explore!"

Tyler looked down at the bird on the ground. Then he looked up at Miss Jones. "So we should put it back?"

"Of course, but that's easier said than done," said Miss Jones as she looked up at the tree. "Does anyone see a nest up there?"

Lucas didn't wait for the group to answer. He was already climbing up the lowest branches. Emily said something about not falling and major head injuries as he climbed higher.

"Do be careful, Lucas!" urged Miss Jones.

"Found it!" he announced. "And there are two more babies inside!" Miss Jones gently picked up the bird with a paper towel. Then she passed the little bundle up to Lucas.

With care, Lucas shook the baby bird into the nest.

"Oh, Lucas! What an absolute miracle! I can't believe you pulled that off! Bravo!" exclaimed Miss Jones as Lucas jumped to the ground.

Tyler wanted to say something smart so that Miss Jones would smile at him, too. "It looks like this time a bad thing became a good thing," he said.

TALKING TOGETHER

1. Why do you think a wild bird would rather be free, even if his life would be safer if he stayed inside a cage?

2. How is a bird being free to live in the wild the same as God allowing us to make our own decisions, including mistakes?

3. Why does God want us to be happy and safe?

4. Where is God when we are happy? Scared? Mad? Thankful? Hurt?

5. Where does God want us to be when we are happy? Scared? Mad? Thankful? Hurt?

ACTIVITY CORNER

Choose a song that has both slow and fast tempos. Sit opposite one other person. Do a simple hand clapping pattern together to match the beat of the song. One pattern can be clapping your own hands and then clapping each other's.

The slow parts of the song can represent hard times. Just like your clapping partner, God always moves with us even when times are hard.

God is also with us and shares our joy when we are happy, which can be represented with a faster beat. In the Bible story there was probably dancing with hand clapping at the party.

Think about it: It is the father who throws the party for his returning son. Do you think that God celebrates when we step off the path and then come back?

GOD TRANSFORMS US

CHAPTER 7

WHAT WE WANT KIDS TO KNOW:

- **God offers us opportunities to turn away from doing bad things and to do good things.**
- **This good is communal as well as personal.**
- **We, in turn, can work for the good of others.**

THE BASICS FOR PARENTS & TEACHERS

Our Bible story about Saul's transformation on the road to Damascus will be heard in a concrete way by the children. But as adults we should be aware of the spiritual significance of the story as well.

At the beginning of the story, Saul was full of negative, destructive energy. When the blindness came upon him, it was not only physical but spiritual as well. His anger toward the followers of Jesus has blinded him to that which was good. When he experienced a spiritual vision of Jesus, followed by a physical inability to see, Saul was literally stopped in his tracks. Now he had to be guided by others, and he began to "see" inwardly in a reorientation of his life.

Ananias, the other character in this story, was also transformed. He had to overcome his fear and distrust of Saul in order to heal the man. Change was not easy for either Saul or Ananias. But their openness to God's call ended up changing both of their lives. Through Ananias, Saul saw a new future opening up before him. Through Saul, Ananias learns not to prejudge or to fear, but to trust God with the new thing that is before him. Because both men were open to creative transformation, God was able to greatly expand the church.

In telling this story to children, emphasize the fact that both men had to change, and that change wasn't easy. God used the changes to make good things happen. Change happens to everyone because life is a dynamic process, never staying exactly the same. Sometimes the changes are sudden; more often, the changes are gradual. But in both cases, change offers new opportunities that God will use toward our good, and toward the good of others.

Sometimes the change offered to us is to grow in our faith by seeing God's good work in unexpected places. Sometimes it is to dare to reach out to do good beyond the circles in which we are comfortable. In any case, the change offered by God through new circumstances can lead to a breakthrough in the kind of person we are and the kind of person we can become. Change can be an opportunity for the creative power of God to work transformations in us.

THE BIBLE STORY
ACTS 9:1-20 SAUL CHANGES

After the death and Resurrection of Jesus, Jesus' followers worked even harder to spread the good news about Jesus. But there were many people who did not like this new "religion." These people believed that the persons who followed Jesus were wrong and needed to be put straight. Saul was one of those people. In fact, he did his very best to stamp out Christianity altogether.

Saul lived in Jerusalem. He was a very important man. He heard that there were many Christians in Damascus (a city in Syria to the north). He decided to go there. Saul felt that it was his duty to put a stop to this new religion. Saul went to the high priest in Jerusalem. He asked for written authority to go to Damascus and hunt down these "Christians." He would arrest them, and bring them back to Jerusalem.

With papers in hand, Saul and his body guards set out for Damascus. Suddenly a bright light surrounded Saul. He fell to the ground in total astonishment. Then Saul heard a voice coming from the light, "Saul, why are you so cruel to me?"

"Who are you?" Saul asked.

"I am Jesus, the one you are so cruel to," said the voice. "Now go into Damascus. Wait there. You will be told what to do."

The men who were traveling with Saul were speechless. They had heard the voice, but they didn't see anyone or anything. Then, as Saul stood up, he discovered that he could not see.

"What am I going to do now?" Saul asked himself. Now, instead of going into Damascus as a powerful man, Saul had to be led by the hand into the city by his body guards. For three days Saul waited. He did not eat or drink anything. He just waited to find out what he was to do next.

As it happened there was a man living in Damascus whose name was Ananias. Ananias was a follower of Jesus. A vision came to him as well. "Go to the house of Judas on Straight Street. Ask for a man named Saul. You will find him there praying. In a vision he has seen you come to him and place your hands on his eyes so that he might see again."

"Oh," said Ananias, "Lord! I have heard about this man. I have heard about all the harm he has done to your followers in Jerusalem! Now he has come to Damascus to arrest every Christian that he can find. Why should I help him?"

"Go," said the Lord, "and do as I have told you. I have chosen this man to tell many people of Israel about me. He will suffer much for my name." So Ananias went to the house where Saul was. Ananias placed his hands on him.

"Brother Saul," said Ananias, "the Lord Jesus, who appeared

to you on the road as you were coming here, has sent me so that you may see again and be filled with the Holy Spirit." Instantly, Saul was able to see again. He asked Ananias to baptize him. Then he ate some food, regaining his strength.

Saul spent several days with the Christians in Damascus. While he was there, he preached in the synagogues that Jesus is the Son of God. All who heard him were amazed at how he had changed.

God sent Saul to take the good news about Jesus to persons who lived throughout the Roman empire. Saul helped to start many churches. Because he was a Roman citizen, Saul also had a Roman name. When he wrote letters to the new churches, he used this name. Paul's letters are now part of the New Testament. We call these letters "Epistles."

TALKING TOGETHER

1. What kind of changes happened in Saul's life?

2. How did the other people in the story help Saul change his life?

3. How did God help Saul to change his life?

4. What sort of change happened to Ananias?

5. Did Saul's change help other people to change for the better too? How?

THE NEW GIRL

"Class!" announced Mrs. Davis as she led Prudence to the front of the room. "Class!" she tried again as the noisy Sunday school students slowly stopped their activities. "I would like everyone to meet our new girl–"

At that very moment a tall, older woman in a flowing orange gown entered the room. The kids instantly focused their attention on her.

"It's time," said the woman. "Please come quickly, since Harold is anxious to start rehearsal straight away!"

Everyone seemed to forget about meeting Prudence, which she was grateful for. The last thing Prudence wanted was to be introduced as the new kid and then have everyone laugh at her oddball name. She slipped away from the teacher and tried to blend in with the other children as they walked to the sanctuary.

A small, dark-haired boy stepped over alongside her.

"My name is Lucas," he said and then pointed to a girl skipping behind them, "And this weirdo is Emily."

"I am NOT a weirdo!" said Emily as she gave Lucas a playful shove.

Prudence didn't like the way these two kids seemed to know each other well. It made her feel even more like an outsider.

"So what's your name?" Lucas asked. A few uncomfortable moments passed as she struggled to overcome her shyness. The idea came to Prudence that she wouldn't say anything at all.

"Maybe she can't talk," said Emily.

Thankfully, both Emily and Lucas lost interest in her as they entered the church. A full choir was singing scales in beautiful harmony. At the altar, a dozen or so elderly dancers in brightly-colored robes were stretching in graceful movements. One of them, a man in a brilliant blue robe, moved toward the children.

"Let me take a look," he said, surveying them. Then he placed his hand on first Lucas and then Emily and Prudence. "You three will do perfectly," he announced.

Prudence's eyes widened in dismay, but she did not break her vow of silence. "The rest of you will be waving these red veils," continued the man, who was evidently Mr. Harold, the dance director. He then explained to Lucas, Emily and Prudence in a very no nonsense voice how they would be hoisted around by dancers.

As soon as he turned to work with the rest of the boys and girls, Emily and Lucas whispered quietly to each other about their fate. Prudence crept closer to hear what they were saying.

"As long as Mrs. Whitby doesn't have to lift me, I'll be happy," Emily murmured. She was gesturing to a dancer who was not as slim as the others. Prudence wished she could ask what was so bad about being lifted by Mrs. Whitby, but felt trapped by her own decision not to talk.

"Is everyone ready in their places?" called Harold loudly.

The organist started a tune that Prudence recognized from her old church. It was a comforting sound, but now Mrs. Whitby was stepping towards her. "Hold steady now. I've got you," she said kindly as she clasped firm hands around Prudence's waist.

"And God will raise you up on eagle's wings!" sang the choir. Prudence gasped as Mrs. Whitby lifted her up and everything below was suddenly seen from a new perspective.

The swirling scarves seemed to float magically among the graceful dancers. "Make you to shine like the sun!" came the choir's strong voices. A shaft of colorful sunlight was shining through the stained glass windows.

"Oh!" cried Prudence.

"Oh!" echoed Mrs. Whitby, startled by Prudence's gasp.

"She CAN talk!" exclaimed Emily."

The choir director stopped the music. "Is something wrong?" he asked.

Everyone looked at Prudence who was being lowered down gently by Mrs. Whitby.

"It, it was just, kind of neat," she explained shyly.

Everyone seemed to love her answer. All the kids laughed as if Prudence had made a very clever joke. Prudence found herself laughing along with them. Mrs. Whitby gave her a hug and Prudence squeezed her back. Mr. Harold, who had been so stern before, suddenly beamed.

"This is **exactly** the kind of feeling we want all of you to have!" he said with delight.

Prudence, smiling now, stood at the starting position again with Lucas and Emily.

"That was really funny!" said Emily. "So what is your name anyway?"

Prudence waited half a beat to answer. It suddenly occurred to her how this was a chance to be called whatever name she wanted. Some people had called her Prudy, but that was almost as bad as Prudence. Her middle name was April. She had always liked the sound of that name so much better.

"April," she said to Lucas and Emily. "My name is April."

TALKING TOGETHER

1. Why do you think Prudence decided not to talk ?

2. Have you ever made a decision about something and then realized it was a bad idea?

3. Why do you think Prudence decided to start talking and be friends with the other children?

4. How did their attitude toward her and including her influence her decision?

5. Who has helped you become part of the group when you were feeling on the outside?

6. How do you think Prudence's attitude affected how the kids treated her at first?

- Gather several pennies. Pick out the dirtiest ones and talk about the experiences these pennies may have gone through. Pour a half cup of white vinegar into a glass. Add one teaspoonful of salt. Stir. Invite one of the children to dip the dirty penny half-way into the liquid for about 30 seconds.

  Ask the boys and girls what happened to the penny. Then talk about how the vinegar made the penny bright and shiny, just like new again. Talk about how God can help make even old, painful situations bright and new again. God always gives hope for making things better, not just for us, but for everyone. Clean all the pennies and let the children share the pennies with others.

- Build a tower with craft sticks or blocks. Then try removing one piece from the middle. See how this makes it harder for the other pieces to keep the building from falling apart. If too many pieces are taken away, the tower collapses.

  Use these talking points: God wants all of us to be good and strong, and help one another. When we help each other, it is better for us, too. If we help each other, our world can be a better place.

TALKING TO GOD

CHAPTER 8

WHAT WE WANT KIDS TO KNOW:

- **Prayer is how we open ourselves to God's influence on our lives.**
- **God uses our prayers to bring about good possibilities in the world.**
- **There are many forms of prayer.**

THE BASICS FOR PARENTS & TEACHERS

Children start life in a self-centered way. They consider their world by what effect it will have on them. For them, prayer is a means to get what they want. If their prayer fails to deliver the expected results, they assume: 1) they did not pray hard enough or believe strongly enough; 2) the request was not in accordance with God's Grand Plan (which means very little to them). We must give children a more realistic understanding of prayer and what it really is.

Prayer is **not** a way to tell God what to do. After reading "The History Test" on page 86, you might ask the children, "Can we use prayer to do all the work for us?" Of course the answer is no. This leads to the next question: "So what good is prayer?" Prayer is also not telling God what we think God ought to do. Sometimes those requests are simply not possible in this world. Praying for a dead bird will not bring it back to life.

Knowing this, we continually pray for things that cannot happen. But in light of this, God can still use our prayers to bring about other related things that **can** happen. Through God, there are always possibilities for the good, no matter what our circumstances. Prayer opens us to those possibilities, even when we are unwittingly praying for things that cannot happen. Through prayer, we open ourselves to be joined with God's love for the world. In our openness to God's love, God can then use us more effectively in accomplishing good—even when we had not anticipated ahead of time what that good would be.

The prayer with which most Christians are familiar is called the Lord's prayer. This prayer is both an individual prayer and a communal one. The prayer allows us as individuals to name God as parent. Then as part of the community, we hallow God's name. We do this when we reflect God's everlasting love in the way we live our lives.

The next parts of the prayer are for the things we need to help us live the first part of the prayer: health for our bodies through food ("give us this day our daily bread) and health for our souls from God's forgiveness for the things we do wrong ("forgive us our trespasses"). Then because God forgives us, we are also expected to forgive others ("as we forgive those who trespass against us").

Finally, we ask for God's help to keep us from even wanting to do wrong ("lead us not into temptation"). This physical and spiritual health strengthens us, so that God's goodness, or love, will shine on earth through us.

Children often conclude their prayers with a list of "blessings." It is a way of joining in God's love for others with the desire that those we ask God to bless shall experience God's love within their own lives. In some children, this list can grow rather lengthy. One of the reasons for closing prayers with "in Jesus' name we pray" is because we acknowledge that we ourselves do not know the fullness of any situation for which we pray. This closing is a way of releasing the prayers to God's fuller knowledge and love, confident that God will use the prayers according to God's own wisdom.

Luke 6:12-14

One day Jesus went up into the mountainside to pray. He spent the whole night up there, praying to God, and when morning came, he came down and called all his disciples to him. There were many disciples who followed him, but this time he chose just twelve of them to be apostles, so that he could send them out to teach as Jesus himself taught.

Luke 9:10-17

Jesus took his apostles with him to a town. When the crowds heard that he was there, they went there, too, so that they might hear Jesus teach. Jesus welcomed them, and spoke to them for a long time. He also healed some of the people who were sick. The day went by quickly, and the apostles began to worry. It would soon be dark, and there were so many people—they would be getting hungry, and would need a place to stay. So the apostles went up to Jesus, and told him to send the people away so they could find something in the villages nearby.

"You give them something to eat," said Jesus. The apostles were astounded—all they had between them were just five loaves of bread and two pieces of fish. That wouldn't begin to feed all these people! But Jesus told the apostles to have all the people—there were about 5,000 of them!—sit in groups of about fifty each. The disciples did this, and the people all sat down as they were directed, and all the time the disciples were worried about what would happen next.

But Jesus took the loaves of bread and the two fish, looked up to heaven, and gave thanks to God for this food. And then he began breaking the bread and fish into pieces, and handing it to the disciples to give to the people. To the astonishment of everybody,

Jesus kept giving…and giving…and giving, and there always seemed to be more, no matter how much he gave away. Everybody got enough to eat! And afterwards, the disciples even gathered up twelve basketsful of leftovers. What a meal!

Luke 11:1-4

One day Jesus was praying in a certain place. When he finished, one of his disciples said to him, "Lord, teach us to pray, just as John taught his disciples." Jesus said to them all, "When you pray, say 'Father, may we keep your name holy in our hearts and lives, and may we live as you would have us to live, so that earth is like your kingdom in heaven. Give us each day our daily food, and forgive us the things we do wrong. And may we also forgive those who do wrong to us! Keep us from the things that would tempt us to do wrong. Amen."

TALKING TOGETHER

1. In the first story, Jesus spends a long time praying. Do you think he was talking that whole time? Do you think God was talking to him, so that it was like a conversation? Maybe it was some time talking, and some time being open to God's presence with him. How do you think this time of praying made a difference to whom he chose to be his apostles? One of those chosen ones was Judas, who would betray him. Do you think Jesus made a mistake to choose Judas, even after all that prayer?

2. In the second story, the prayer is just a small part of the larger story. The prayer is when Jesus thanks God for the bread and fish. He was "saying grace." The food, which was such a small amount, was somehow enough to feed everybody. Why do we thank God for our food? It usually doesn't multiply, the way it did in this story. Sometimes people really don't have enough food to stay healthy, but still they thank God for what they have. Why do we thank God for what we have, even when it's not enough?

3. Jesus teaches us to pray. The first part of the prayer asks us to remember God's goodness and for help to live good lives ourselves. The next parts of the prayer are for the things we need to help us live the first part of the prayer. We make God's name holy by living this prayer.

A STORY FOR TODAY — PRAYER CHANGES THINGS

Mrs. Roberts was having a hard time keeping the class quiet. The girls and boys were playing with the puppets they had just made. Emily's puppet was hitting Tyler's puppet on the head.

"So what have we learned about prayer?!" said Mrs. Roberts, raising her voice to get everyone's attention.

"Prayer is talking to God!" Emily yelled over the noise.

"Is that all?" shouted back Mrs. Roberts.

Lucas stopped throwing his puppet in the air and said, "Prayer changes things!"

"Yes!" said Mrs. Roberts with relief as she looked at her watch. The class was now over. "I'll see you all next week."

Lucas grabbed Tyler by the arm and ran toward the playground. He came to a stop in the far corner next to the bushes.

"What?" asked Tyler.

Lucas took something out of his coat pocket and held it out

to Tyler. It was a dead baby bird. Tyler's heart dropped. Could this be the same bird they had tried to rescue a few weeks ago?

"Where did you find it?" Tyler asked.

"Under the tree," said Lucas, "but it may not be the same one. I'm thinking we can save this bird too!

"What?!" asked Tyler again.

Lucas looked directly into his friends eyes. "If both of us really, really believe and pray very hard to God, maybe this little bird will get better."

"But, Lucas, it's dead," Tyler said.

Lucas took a deep breath, "We've got to believe and pray!" Both boys bowed their heads. Lucas prayed for God to heal the bird. When the boys opened their eyes again, the bird was still dead.

"Our prayer didn't work. It didn't change anything," said Tyler.

Lucas wasn't ready to give up. "Of course something has changed," he said excitedly. "I can just feel it! Maybe what we need to do now is get the whole church to pray!"

Tyler wasn't comfortable with this idea, but he knew there was no stopping Lucas now. Lucas put the bird back in his pocket. The two boys went to find their families. Tyler would sit with Lucas and his family during worship.

The pastor came to the part of the service where the congregation identified any concerns to be included in their prayer that day. Tyler hoped that Lucas had forgotten about the dead bird. But no such luck. Lucas raised his hand up high.

"Yes?" asked the pastor, bringing the microphone close to where Lucas was sitting. At that point Lucas' bravery went away. "Um, Tyler wants to tell us about something," he muttered.

Tyler's mouth dropped open. How could he possibly ask everyone to pray for a dead bird? He stood up and gave Lucas a scowl. Then he saw his parents smiling encouragingly at him.

"I, uh, I wanted to ask everyone to pray for ...uh, Lucas' grandmother. She's... in the hospital," he stammered, surprised that words were actually coming out of his mouth. There were murmurs of concern from the congregation. And the pastor moved on.

After church, Tyler's parents suggested that both families go out to lunch. Then they could all go to the hospital to see Lucas' grandmother.

At the hospital that afternoon, Lucas told his grandmother how Tyler had asked the the whole church to pray for her. She reached out her arms to both boys and hugged them.

"I feel protected and loved today," said Lucas' grandmother. "It has to be from the prayers, don't you think!"

"See," said Lucas punching Tyler on the arm. "Ms. Roberts was right about prayer. It does change things!"

Tyler was about to say that not much had changed for the bird, but he didn't want to ruin the moment. Besides, he thought to himself, who was to say what was supposed to change exactly with prayer. It was probably up to God anyway!

1. Why do you think praying doesn't work to change something that has already happened in the past, like praying for a bird not to have died when it is already dead?

2. What if God doesn't use prayers to change what's already happened, but to change how we feel about what's already happened, and guide us toward what we might do about it?

3. How did God use Lucas' prayer for the bird to end up helping his grandmother?

4. How did prayers from the congregation make the grandmother feel better?

5. How sure can we be about what exactly will happen because of our prayers?

6. What does it mean to trust God to handle our prayers in the best way possible?

7 Have you ever asked God for something that you didn't get? Why do you think your prayer was answered in a way different from what you expected?

8 Do you think God ever says "no" or "not now"?

• Use the following recipe to make play dough.

½ cup salt   1 cup flour
1 T. cream of tartar   1 cup water
1 T. vegetable oil   food coloring

Combine ingredients in a saucepan. Cook on low, stirring all the time. When the dough looks like mashed potatoes, take the pan off the stove. Allow the mixture to cool.

Make various shapes with the children. If the world is like this clay mixture, it can be shaped into unlimited possibilities, but it will still always be play dough. It will never be a bicycle or a computer. God works with the world as it is. God brings it to where it can be. When we pray to God. God uses our prayers to bring about what good is really possible for our world.

• Many religions use beads to help direct prayers. Find some craft beads or beads from an old necklace (or create some from the clay in the previous activity). A shoe string or dental floss can be used for stringing, depending on the size of the holes in the beads.

Start with a large or distinctive bead to mark the beginning of the prayer chain. Then add a bead for each prayer, such as one for each member of your family, each of your friends, your church, your school or any other thing you want to pray for. It is a good idea to write down the prayers as well. The beads can be connected like a bracelet or left as a chain. When you pray, touch each bead that represents a specific person or thing.

CHURCH & MISSION

CHAPTER 9

WHAT WE WANT KIDS TO KNOW:

- **The church is a community of persons called to live out the gospel of Jesus Christ in word and deed.**
- **Living the gospel of Jesus Christ means growing in love of God and one another.**

THE BASICS FOR PARENTS & TEACHERS

While the story of Easter often seems to be like a "grand finale" to the story of Jesus, it is actually the point where the story moves from its focus on Christ in the gospels to Christ in the world through the church.

The church is often referred to as "the body of Christ," not simply because it participates in Christ through baptism and the Lord's supper, but because the church is the continuation of Christ's life and work in the world. The book of John makes this especially clear through the imagery of Jesus as the vine and us as the branches (John 15). John also uses language such as "I am in my Father, and you are in me, and I am in you" (John 14:20). "I tell you the truth," said Jesus in John 14:12, "all who have faith in me will do what I have been doing. They will do even greater things than these." The church is the continuation of Jesus' work in the world.

The work of Jesus was and is to reveal God to us. This revelation then transforms how we live our lives. Like Jesus, this love calls forth acts of compassion and caring. John Wesley called this kind of love "sanctification," which means always increasing in love for God and neighbor.

Love is by necessity relational. To love means to be in a caring relationship with others. The body of Christ, then, is a community where we love one another, and build one another up in lives of faith and love. This happens as we worship together, pray together, study together, and support one another. To nurture children in the faith is one of the ways that we live out the love of God. As the body of Christ, we are also called to see to one another's well-being. As we do so, we participate in God's love, for God loves each one of us. We join God in loving.

But God's love is universal—we learned this through Jesus. To be the body of Christ can never be fully authentic if love is restricted to only those who are also within the body of Christ. The church must practice living the love of God in the world beyond its walls. This is what we mean by "mission."

The mission of the church is expressed in Matthew 25, where Jesus calls us to acts of mercy, seeing to the well-being of those who are in trouble. Another passage in Matthew and also in Mark summarizes this in a different way, by telling us to "give a cup of cold water" in Christ's name (Matthew 10:42; Mark 9:41).

Our acts of kindness, whether corporate, in relief agencies, or personal, in reaching out to a neighbor, are in the name of Christ. This is why the final Matthew passage gives the church a teaching mission that will lead others to become disciples. When the church does this, it is entering into the love of God as revealed in Jesus. We offer words of mercy as well as acts of mercy, continuing the revelation that has been given to us all in Jesus Christ our Lord. In doing so, we are the church, the Body of Christ.

The gospel of John tells us what Jesus said to his disciples the night before he was put to death on the cross:

As God has loved me, so have I loved you. Now remain in my love. If you obey my commands, you will remain in my love, just as I have obeyed God's commands and remain in God's love. I have told you this so that my joy may be in you, and that your joy may be complete.

My command is this: Love each other as I have loved you. Greater love has no one than this, that he gives his life for his friends. I have called you friends, for everything that I learned from God I have made known to you. You didn't choose me, but I chose you, and appointed you to go and bear fruit—fruit that will last. This is my command: love each other.

Matthew 28:16-20

The book of Matthew tells of some of Jesus' very last words to the disciples:

Then the eleven disciples went to Galilee, where Jesus had told them to go. When they saw Jesus there, they worshiped him.

Jesus said, "All authority in heaven and on earth has been given to me. Now I am giving you the authority to go and share what you have learned.

Make disciples throughout the earth. Baptize people in the name of the Father and of the Son and of the Holy Spirit, and teach them to obey everything I have commanded you. And I will be with you always, even to the end of time.

Matthew 25: 32-45

Also in the book of Matthew, Jesus tells a story about how we are to love and serve him in the way we care for others:

When the Son of Man comes into his glory, and all the angels with him, he will sit on a wonderful throne, like a great King. All the people of the earth will be gathered before him, and he will separate the people into two groups, with one group going to his left, and the other to his right.

Then the King will say to those on his right, "Come, you who are blessed by God, and take the goodness God has prepared for you. When I was hungry, you gave me something to eat. When I was thirsty, you gave me something to drink. I was a stranger and you invited me in. I needed clothes and you gave me some. I was sick and you took care of me. I was in prison and you came to visit me."

Then these people will say, "But Lord, when was that? When did we see you hungry, and give you something to eat, or thirsty, and give you something to drink? When did we see you a stranger, and invite you in, or needing clothes, and give you some? When did we see you sick or in prison, and go to visit you?"

The king will reply, "I tell you the truth, whatever you did for anyone who was in need, no matter how great or small, it was as though you did for me."

TALKING TOGETHER

1. How do we know that God loves us?

2. How does God know that we love God?

3. If God loves everybody, and we love God, can we love everybody too? How would that happen?

4. Some things are too big for only one or two people to do. Think about how the church with many people can do things that one person has trouble doing on his or her own. Could this be what Jesus meant when he told his disciples, "You will do greater things than me"?

5. What are some of the ways that we tell the story of God's love?

A STORY FOR TODAY — THE DANCE

Emily's heart was racing. Why had she let herself be talked into doing a tap dance at the nursing home? With dread she followed the other church members who had volunteered to participate in the show.

Emily tried not to look into the open rooms on either side of the hallway. It was just depressing. Some of the nursing home residents were lying on low beds in there. And it didn't smell very good either.

"There you are!" her dance partner April said, as she came over to meet Emily. Next to April was an old woman in a wheelchair.

"Hello!" the woman said to Emily. "I'm Pauline. My, don't you look nice!"

"Hello," said Emily politely, glad that at least Pauline seemed **normal**.

Another nearby nursing home resident was holding a glass of water in her hand and looking very grumpy. "What do you have to do around here for a glass of water!" she demanded angrily.

"Oh, don't mind Laura," said Pauline. "She's usually on the third floor, but the staff brought her down today for your show. Laura used to be a tap-dancer too, so I know she's going to love seeing you." An aide, meanwhile, stepped over and tried to help her.

"Look! Look!" a woman with a walker said, pointing at Emily and April. "Oh you look just like I did on performance night!" Emily couldn't help but feel a small glow of pride.

"What do you have to do to get a glass of water around here!" yelled Laura.

A man whose nametag identified him as the Activities Director approached. "It's show time," he said.

Emily took a deep breath and the two girls joined the large gathering in the dining hall. The place was filled with people in wheelchairs. Behind the chairs were the nursing home workers and other visitors from church.

"Don't be discouraged if you see a few people sleeping in the audience," said the Activities Director. "Just know that we all appreciate you being here!"

Pastor Linda was now introducing the show with a prayer. She ended with, "Through everyone here, lead us into creating a moment of joy and praise for your goodness, Amen."

Who could think about joy in a place like this? thought Emily.

After the first act, a men's quartet, the church members gave a loud round of applause. There was only a weak response from the nursing home residents. Emily soon saw that this was the applause pattern for all the acts. She and April were to perform last.

"You ready?" asked April as their music began to play. There was a rustle among the wheelchairs as April clicked her way across the stage area. Emily followed, keeping a show smile pasted to her face. She could see that grumpy Laura was in the front row, now clasping two glasses of water. Full attention, rather than anger, was her expression. Someone started clapping to the music and soon the whole room was in rhythm to their tapping shoes. Instead of feeling stiff and afraid, Emily felt herself relax. After the final note, a definite applause sounded from the wheelchair section with shouts of "More! More!" Emily noticed that an old gentleman in a worn suit had his hand on Laura's shoulder.

"Thank you!" shouted Pastor Linda over the noise as she came up to the front clapping. Emily was turning to go with April when the gentlemen who was with Laura touched her arm. Emily looked up in alarm.

"I want to give a special thank you for what you did today," he said. There were tears in his eyes. Emily thought at first someone must have told him how scared she was of nursing homes.

"It really wasn't so bad," she started, but he kept on talking.

"My wife Laura used to love dancing, so I know it meant so much to her to see your performance. Thank you for bringing her this happiness."

"We love dancing," Laura said, looking up at the man. This visibly choked him up even more.

"Thank you," he managed to say again and then wheeled Laura away. Emily stood there, feeling slightly stunned. It had never occurred to her that helping cranky, demented Laura would seem as important as it did now. If Emily could connect with someone in a place she had been so afraid of, it made her think of how many other possibilities there must be to connect with all kinds of people everywhere.

1. Why did the Sunday school class come to the nursing home?

2. How did this show the love of Christ?

3. How does this story remind you of things that were said in the Bible stories?

4. How does your church reach out to people who need to know the love of God?

5. How do you show the love of God by connecting to people in need?

ACTIVITY CORNER

Make a list with the children of charity organizations that your church (or any local church) supports. This may involve reading through a newsletter, website or calling the Pastor. As you learn about the different organizations, find out which one interests your group the most. Explore ways the children could be involved in or contribute to this mission.

- Explain to the children how the church is more than a building. A church is a group of people who actively try to grow in ways to be more like Jesus and to help others in the world.

Take a potato and show how instead of just being a vegetable on its own, the potato can grow to have beautiful green leaves and can even be planted to make new potatoes.

First cut off a few inches from one end. Then stick some toothpicks in the potato to support it over a glass jar filled with water. Place the cut side down in the water, and put the jar in a sunny location. Make sure the water level doesn't dip below the cut end of the potato.

Carrots are another root vegetable that can be grown inside. Cut off the top one inch of a carrot. If it's still green inside, it will grow. Set the cut top in a shallow bowl of water so that the water just covers the base and allows the top to stay above the surface. In a week or so you'll see new growth. Keep the water topped off so the carrot doesn't dry out.

96